Learn to do
Bavarian
Crochet ™

Contents

Special Stitches

Treble (tr): See Stitch Guide.

Front post treble (fptr): See Stitch Guide.

Large Shell (lg shell): (4 tr, {ch 1, 4 tr} twice) in place indicated.

Small Shell (sm shell): (4 tr, ch 1, 4 tr) in place indicated.

4-treble cluster (4-tr cl): Holding last lp of each st on hook (*see photo 1*), 4 tr in place indicated, yo, pull through all lps on hook (*see photo 2*).

4-back post treble decrease (4-bptr dec): Holding back last lp of each st on hook, **bptr** (*see Stitch Guide*) around each of next 4 sts, yo, pull through all lps on hook (*see photo 3*).

The 4-bptr dec is always worked on a 4-tr group of the same shell.

8-back post treble decrease (8-bptr dec):

Holding back last lp of each st on hook, bptr around each of next 4 sts, sk sc between shells and working on next shell, rep between * once, yo, pull through all lps on hook.

The 8-bptr dec is always worked using the last 4-tr group of 1 shell and the first 4-tr group of the next shell (see photo 4).

If you find it difficult to hold all of the stitches on your hook when working the 8-bptr dec, you might try using an afghan or double-ended hook for added length.

Photo 4

HOW TO MAKE A BASIC SQUARE USED IN BAVARIAN SQUARE AFGHAN, SHRUG AND BAG.

Rnd 1: With first color, ch 5, sl st in first ch to form ring, ch 1, [sc in ring, ch 5, **4-tr cl** (see *Special Stitches*) in ring, ch 5] 4 times (see *photo 1*), join with sl st in beg sc (see *photo 2*). (8 ch-5 sps, 4 sc, 4 4-tr cls)

Photo 1

Photo 2

Join with slip stitch as indicated unless otherwise stated.

First ch of ch-5 made after working either a cluster or a bptr dec is actually the "locking stitch." This ch forms the "o" at the top of the stitch that will be worked into on the next row or rnd.

Working into the "top" of the stitch in this manner forms the appearance that all of the stitches of both the shell and the cluster or decrease are worked in the same place. If you work the shell in the wrong place, it will change the way the center of the square looks (see *top of st photo*).

Top of Stitch Photo

For ease in counting, the first ch of the ch-5 after a cluster or decrease is not included as part of the cluster or decrease, but is counted as part of the ch-5, even though you will be using it as the "top" of the stitch when working the next row or rnd.

Rnd 2: Ch 1, sc in first sc, ch 2, **lg shell** *(see Special Stitches)* in top of next 4-tr cl *(see photo 3)*, ch 2, [sc in next sc, ch 2, lg shell in top of next 4-tr cl, ch 2] 3 times, join in beg sc *(see photo 4)*. Fasten off. *(8 ch-2 sps, 4 large shells, 4 sc)*

Ch-2 sps are used in rnd 2 only to add height. They will not be worked into or used on any subsequent rnds. Piece may ruffle slightly until next rnd is worked.

Rnd 3: Join next color with sc in first ch-1 sp on any shell, ch 5, **4-bptr dec** *(see Special Stitches)*, ch 5, sc in next ch-1 sp of shell, ch 5, **8-bptr dec** *(see Special Stitches)*, ch 5, [sc in next ch-1 sp of shell, ch 5, 4-bptr dec, ch 5, sc in next ch-1 sp of shell, ch 5, 8-bptr dec, ch 5] 3 times, join in beg sc *(see photo 5)*. *(8 sc, 4 8-bptr dec, 4 4-bptr dec)*

Photo 3

Photo 4

Photo 5

Rnd 4: Ch 1, sc in first sc, lg shell in top of the next 4-bptr dec (see Top of Stitch photo page 6) before rnd 2, sc in next sc, **sm shell** (see Special Stitches) in top of next 8-bptr dec, [sc in next sc, lg shell in top of the next 4-bptr dec, sc in next sc, sm shell in top of next 8-bptr dec] 3 times, join in beg sc (see photo 6). Fasten off. (4 lg shells, 4 sm shells)

Photo 6

Rnd 5: Join next color with sc in first ch-1 sp of any large shell, *ch 5, 4-bptr dec, ch 5, sc in next ch-1 sp, ch 5, 8-bptr dec, ch 5, sc in next ch-1 sp, ch 5, work 8-bptr dec, ch 5**, sc in next ch-1 sp, rep from * around, ending last rep at **, join in beg sc (see photo 7). (4 4-bptr dec, 8 8-bptr dec, 12 sc)

Rnd 6: Ch 1, sc in first sc, *lg shell in top of next 4-bptr dec, sc in next sc, sm shell in top of next 8-bptr dec, sc in next sc, sm shell in top of next 8-bptr dec**, sc in next sc, rep from * around, ending last rep at **, join in beg sc. Fasten off. (4 lg shells, 8 sm shells)

Rnd 7: Join next color with sc in first ch-1 sp of any corner shell, *ch 5, 4-bptr dec, ch 5, sc in next ch-1 sp, ch 5, 8-bptr dec, ch 5, sc in next ch-1 sp, ch 5, 8-bptr dec, ch 5, sc in next ch-1 sp, ch 5, 8-bptr dec, ch 5**, sc in next ch-1 sp, rep from * around, ending last rep at **, join in beg sc.

Rnd 8: Ch 1, sc in first sc, *lg shell in top of next 4-bptr dec, sc in next sc, sm shell in top of next 8-bptr dec, sc in next sc, sm shell in top of next 8-bptr dec, sc in next sc, small shell in top of next 8-bptr dec**, sc in next sc, rep from * around, ending last rep at **, join in beg sc. Fasten off. (4 lg shells, 12 sm shells)

Next rnds: To make the square larger, continue repeating rnds 7 and 8 alternately, working 2 rnds of each color until square is the desired size. You will be adding 1 sm shell to each side of square with every 2 rnds worked.

To vary the texture and look of the square, you may choose to turn at the end of each rnd as is done in the Gilded Edge Table Runner. To do this, simply turn your work at the end of each round, then work the first sc in the top of the joining sc of the last rnd.

Photo 7

HOW TO MAKE A BASIC TRIANGLE USED IN SHAWL.

Row 1: Starting at center of long edge on triangle, with first color, ch 6, **lg shell** (*see Special Stitches*) in 6th ch from hook, ch 1, tr in same ch as lg shell, **turn**. Fasten off (*see photo 1*).

Photo 1

Ch-5 left at beg of row 1 counts as first tr and ch-1 sp. When working lg shell, insert hook under both top lps of ch to avoid stretching ch and forming an unsightly hole.

Row 2: Join next color with sc in first tr, sk next ch-1 sp, ch 5, **4-bptr dec** (*see Special Stitches*) across first 4 sts of shell, ch 5, sc in next ch-1 sp, ch 5, 4-bptr dec across next 4 sts of shell, ch 5, sc in next ch-1 sp, ch 5, 4-bptr dec across last 4 sts of shell, ch 1, tr in 4th ch of ch-5 (*see photo 2*), turn. (*3 4-bptr dec, 3 sc, 1 tr*)

Photo 2

Row 3: Ch 4 (*counts as first tr*), **sm shell** (*see Special Stitches*) in top of next 4-bptr dec, sc in next sc, lg shell in top of next 4-bptr dec, sc in next sc, sm shell in top of next 4-bptr dec, ch 1, tr in last tr, turn (*see photo 3*). Fasten off. (*2 sm shells, 1 lg shell*)

Photo 3

Row 4: Join next color with sc in first tr, ch 5, 4-bptr dec, ch 5, sc in next ch-1 sp, ch 5, **8-bptr dec** (*see Special Stitches*), ch 5, sc in next ch-1 sp, ch 5, 4-bptr dec (*center point*), ch 5, sc in next ch-1 sp, ch 5, 8-bptr dec, ch 5, sc in next ch-1 sp, ch 5, 4-bptr dec, tr in top of ch-4 (*see photo 4*), turn.

Photo 4

Row 5: Ch 4, sm shell in top of first 4-bptr dec, sc in next sc, sm shell in top of next 8-bptr dec, sc in next sc, lg shell in top of next 4-bptr dec *(center point)*, sc in next sc, sm shell in top of next 8-bptr dec, sc in next sc, sm shell in top of last 4-bptr dec, tr in last ch-5 sp, turn. Fasten off *(see photo 5).* *(4 sm shells, 1 lg shell)*

Photo 5

Row 6: Join next color with sc in first tr, ch 5, 4-bptr dec, ch 5, [sc in next ch-1 sp, ch 5, 8-bptr dec, ch 5] twice, sc in next ch-1 sp, ch 5, 4-bptr dec, ch 5, [sc in next ch-1 sp, ch 5, 8-bptr dec, ch 5] twice, sc in next ch-1 sp, ch 5, 4-bptr dec, tr in top of ch-4, turn.

Row 7: Ch 4, sm shell in top of first 4-bptr dec, sc in next sc, [sm shell in top of next 8-bptr dec, sc in next sc] twice, lg shell in top of next 4-bptr dec, sc in next sc, [sm shell in top of next 8-bptr dec, sc in next sc] twice, sm shell in top of last 4-bptr dec, tr in last ch-5 sp, turn. Fasten off. *(6 sm shells, 1 lg shell)*

Next rows: To make the triangle larger, continue repeating rows 6 and 7 alternately, working 2 rows of each color until triangle is desired size. You will be adding one sm shell to each side of triangle with every 2 rows worked.

HOW TO MAKE A BASIC RECTANGLE
USED IN TABLE RUNNER, BABY AFGHAN AND SHRUG.
SMALL RECTANGLE

When working into beg ch, insert hook under top 2 lps of ch to avoid stretching ch and leaving an unsightly hole.

Be careful when counting sk chs after working sm shell, as it is easy to miss the first ch after the shell.

Rnd 1: With first color, ch 22, sc in 2nd ch from hook, [sk next 4 chs, **sm shell** (see Special Stitches) in next ch, sk next 4 chs, sc in next ch] twice (see photo 1), working on opposite side of starting ch, sk first 5 chs, sm shell in next ch which will be the same ch as sm shell on opposite side of ch (see photo 2), sk next 4 chs, sc in next ch, sk next 4 chs, sm shell in next ch which will be the same ch as sm shell on opposite side, sk last 5 chs, join in beg sc (see photo 3). Fasten off. (4 sc, 4 small shells)

Photo 3

Rnd 2: Join next color with sc in first sc, *ch 5, **4-bptr dec** (see Special Stitches), ch 5, sc in next ch-1 sp, ch 5, **8-bptr dec** (see Special Stitches), ch 5, sc in next ch-1 sp, ch 5, 4-bptr dec, ch 5*, sc in next sc, rep between * once, join in beg sc (see photo 4). (6 sc, 2 8-bptr dec, 4 4-bptr dec)

Photo 1

Photo 2

Photo 4

Rnd 3: Ch 1, sc in first sc, **lg shell** (see Special Stitches) in top of first 4-bptr dec (corner), sc in next sc, sm shell in top of next 8-bptr dec, sc in next sc, lg shell in top of next 4-bptr dec (corner), sc in next sc, lg shell in top of next 4-bptr dec (corner), sc in next sc, sm shell in top of next 8-bptr dec, sc in next sc, lg shell in top of last 4-bptr dec (corner), join in beg sc. Fasten off (see photo 5). (6 sc, 4 lg shells, 2 sm shells)

Photo 5

Rnd 4: Join next color with sc in first ch-1 sp of first corner shell, *ch 5, 4-bptr dec, ch 5, sc in next ch-1 sp, [ch 5, 8-bptr dec, ch 5, sc in next ch-1 sp] twice, ch 5, 4-bptr dec, ch 5, sc in next ch-1 sp, ch 5, 8-bptr dec*, ch 5, sc in next ch-1 sp, rep between * once, join in beg sc (see photo 6). (4 4-bptr dec, 6 8-bptr dec, 10 sc)

Photo 6

Rnd 5: Ch 1, sc in first sc, *lg shell in top of next 4-bptr dec, sc in next sc, [sm shell in top of next 8-bptr dec, sc in next sc] twice, lg shell in top of next 4-bptr dec, sc in next sc, sm shell in top of next 8-bptr dec*, sc in next sc, rep between * once, join in beg sc. Fasten off. (4 lg shells, 6 sm shells)

Rnd 6: Join next color with sc in first ch-1 sp of shell in first corner, *ch 5, 4-bptr dec, ch 5, sc in next ch-1 sp, [ch 5, 8-bptr dec, ch 5, sc in next ch-1 sp] 3 times, ch 5, 4-bptr dec, ch 5, [sc in next ch-1 sp, ch 5, 8-bptr dec, ch 5] twice*, sc in next ch-1 sp, rep between * once, join in beg sc. (10 8-bptr dec, 4 4-bptr dec, 14 sc)

Rnd 7: Ch 1, sc in first sc, *lg shell in top of next 4-bptr dec, sc in next sc, [sm shell in top of next 8-bptr dec, sc in next sc] 3 times, lg shell in top of next 4-bptr dec, [sc in next sc, sm shell in top of next 8-bptr dec] twice*, sc in next sc, rep between * once, join in beg sc. Fasten off. (4 large shells, 10 small shells, 14 sc)

Next rnds: To make the rectangle larger, continue repeating rnds 6 and 7 alternately, working 2 rnds of each color. You will be adding 1 sm shell to each side of rectangle with every 2 rnds worked.

To make a longer rectangle, work beg ch in multiples of 10 plus 2 more. Each sm shell rep uses 10 chs. See rnd 1 of Gilded Edge Table Runner on next page and page 43 as an example.

To vary the texture and look of the rectangle, you may choose to turn at the end of each rnd as featured in the Gilded Edge Table Runner. When working in this manner, you will work across a short edge first, then the long edge. On the next rnd, you will again work across the long edge first, then the short edge. ∎

Bavarian
Lullaby

SKILL LEVEL

INTERMEDIATE

FINISHED SIZE
35 x 37 inches

MATERIALS
- Plymouth Dreambaby DK light (light worsted) weight yarn (1¾ oz/183 yds/ 50g per ball):
  - 3 balls each #100 white, #104 yellow, #102 blue, #107 lavender and #105 green
- Size F/5/3.75mm crochet hook or size needed to obtain gauge

GAUGE
2 sm shells and 2 sc = 4 inches; 9 rnds = 4 inches

PATTERN NOTES
See photos for Special Stitches and How-To on pages 4–12.

Join with slip stitch as indicated unless otherwise stated.

SPECIAL STITCHES
4-back post treble decrease (4-bptr dec): Holding back last lp of each st on hook, **bptr** (*see Stitch Guide*) around each of next 4 sts, yo, pull through all lps on hook (*see photo 3 on page 4*).

8-back post treble decrease (8-bptr dec): *Holding back last lp of each st on hook, bptr

around each of next 4 sts*, sk sc between shells and working on next shell, rep between * once, yo, pull through all lps on hook (*see photo 4 on page 5*).

Large shell (lg shell): (4 tr, {ch 1, 4 tr} twice) in place indicated.

Small shell (sm shell): (4 tr, ch 1, 4 tr) in place indicated.

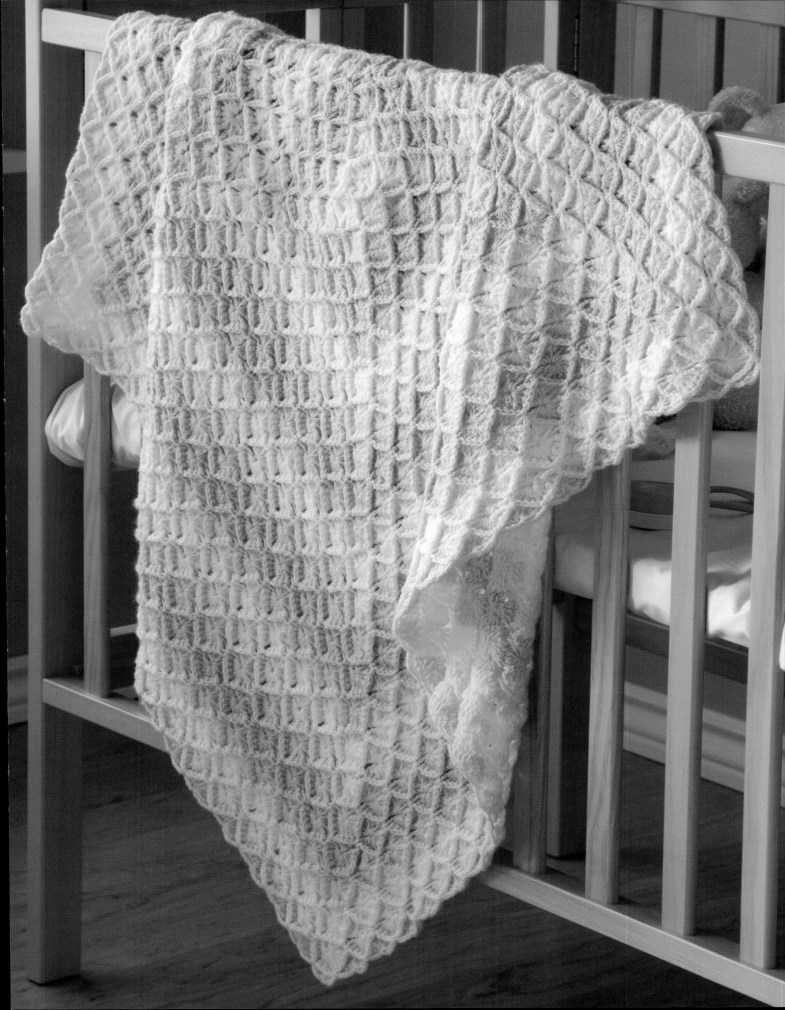

INSTRUCTIONS
AFGHAN

Rnd 1: Beg in center, with white, ch 22, sc in 2nd ch from hook, [sk next 4 chs, **sm shell** (see Special Stitches) in next ch, sk next 4 chs, sc in next ch] twice, working on opposite side of ch, sk first 5 chs, sm shell in next ch (same ch as shell on opposite side of ch), sk next 4 chs, sc in next ch, sk next 4 chs, sm shell in next ch, sk last 5 chs, **join** (see Pattern Notes) in first sc. Fasten off. (4 sc, 4 sm shells)

Rnd 2: Join yellow with sc in first sc, *ch 5, **4-bptr dec** (see Special Stitches), ch 5, sc in next ch-1 sp, ch 5, **8-bptr dec** (see Special Stitches), ch 5, sc in next ch-1 sp, ch 5, 4-bptr dec, ch 5*, sc in next sc, rep between * once, join in beg sc. (6 sc, 2 8-bptr dec, 4 4-bptr dec)

Rnd 3: Ch 1, sc in first sc, **lg shell** (see Special Stitches) in top of first 4-bptr dec (corner), sc in next sc, sm shell in top of next 8-bptr dec, sc in next sc, [lg shell in top of next 4-bptr dec (corner), sc in next sc] twice, sm shell in top of next 8-bptr dec, sc in next sc, lg shell in top of last 4-bptr dec (corner), join in beg sc. Fasten off. (6 sc, 4 lg shells, 2 sm shells)

Rnd 4: Join blue with sc in first ch-1 sp of first corner shell, *ch 5, 4-bptr dec, ch 5, sc in next ch-1 sp, [ch 5, 8-bptr dec, ch 5, sc in next ch-1 sp] twice, ch 5, 4-bptr dec, ch 5, sc in next ch-1 sp, ch 5, work 8-bptr dec*, ch 5, sc in next ch-1 sp, rep between * once, join in beg sc. (4 4-bptr dec, 6 8-bptr dec, 10 sc)

Rnd 5: Ch 1, sc in first sc, *lg shell in top of next 4-bptr dec, sc in next sc, [sm shell in top of next 8-bptr dec, sc in next sc] twice, lg shell in top of next 4-bptr dec, sc in next sc, sm shell in top of next 8-bptr dec*, sc in next sc, rep between * once, join in beg sc. Fasten off. (4 lg shells, 6 sm shells)

Rnd 6: Join lavender with sc in first ch-1 sp of first corner shell, *ch 5, 4-bptr dec, ch 5, sc in next ch-1 sp, [ch 5, 8-bptr dec, ch 5, sc in next ch-1 sp] 3 times, ch 5, 4-bptr dec, ch 5, [sc in next ch-1 sp, ch 5, 8-bptr dec, ch 5] twice*, sc in next ch-1 sp, rep between * once, join in beg sc. (10 8-bptr dec, 4 4-bptr dec, 14 sc)

Rnd 7: Ch 1, sc in first sc, *lg shell in top of next 4-bptr dec, sc in next sc, [sm shell in top of next 8-bptr dec, sc in next sc] 3 times, lg shell in top of next 4-bptr dec, [sc in next sc, sm shell in top of next 8-bptr dec] twice*, sc in next sc, rep between * once, join in beg sc. Fasten off. (4 lg shells, 10 sm shells, 14 sc)

Rnd 8: Join green with sc in first ch-1 sp of any corner shell, *ch 5, 4-bptr dec, ch-5, [sc in next ch-1 sp, ch 5, 8-bptr dec, ch 5] across to next corner**, sc in next ch-1 sp, rep from * around, ending last rep at **, join in beg sc. (4 4-bptr dec, 14 8-bptr dec, 18 sc)

Rnd 9: Ch 1, sc in first sc, *lg shell in top of next 4-bptr dec, [sc in next sc, sm shell in top of next 8-bptr dec] across to next corner**, sc in next sc, rep from * around, ending last rep at **, join in beg sc. Fasten off. (4 lg shells, 14 sm shells, 18 sc)

Rnd 10: Join white with sc in first ch-1 sp of any corner shell, *ch 5, 4-bptr dec, ch-5, [sc in next ch-1 sp, ch 5, 8-bptr dec, ch 5] across to next corner**, sc in next ch-1 sp, rep from * around, ending last rep at **, join in beg sc. (4 4-bptr dec, 18 8-bptr dec, 22 sc)

Rnd 11: Ch 1, sc in first sc, *lg shell in top of next 4-bptr dec, [sc in next sc, sm shell in top of next 8-bptr dec] across to next corner**, sc in next sc, rep from * around, ending last rep at **, join in beg sc. Fasten off. (4 lg shells, 18 sm shells, 22 sc)

Rnd 12: Join yellow with sc in first ch-1 sp of any corner shell, *ch 5, 4-bptr dec, ch-5, [sc in next ch-1 sp, ch 5, 8-bptr dec, ch 5] across to next corner**, sc in next ch-1 sp, rep from * around, ending last rep at **, join in beg sc. *(4 4-bptr dec, 22 8-bptr dec, 26 sc)*

Rnd 13: Ch 1, sc in first sc, *lg shell in top of next 4-bptr dec, [sc in next sc, sm shell in top of next 8-bptr dec] across to next corner**, sc in next sc, rep from * around, ending last rep at **, join in beg sc. Fasten off. *(4 lg shells, 22 sm shells, 26 sc)*

Rnd 14: Join blue with sc in first ch-1 sp of any corner shell, *ch 5, 4-bptr dec, ch-5, [sc in next ch-1 sp, ch 5, 8-bptr dec, ch 5] across to next corner**, sc in next ch-1 sp, rep from * around, ending last rep at **, join in beg sc. *(4 4-bptr dec, 26 8-bptr dec, 30 sc)*

Rnd 15: Ch 1, sc in first sc, *lg shell in top of next 4-bptr dec, [sc in next sc, sm shell in top of next 8-bptr dec] across to next corner**, sc in next sc, rep from * around, ending last rep at **, join in beg sc. Fasten off. *(4 lg shells, 26 sm shells, 30 sc)*

Rnd 16: Join lavender with sc in first ch-1 sp of any corner shell, *ch 5, 4-bptr dec, ch-5, [sc in next ch-1 sp, ch 5, work 8-bptr dec, ch 5] across to next corner**, sc in next ch-1 sp, rep from * around, ending last rep at **, join in beg sc. *(4 4-bptr dec, 30 8-bptr dec, 34 sc)*

Rnd 17: Ch 1, sc in first sc, *lg shell in top of next 4-bptr dec, [sc in next sc, sm shell in top of next 8-bptr dec] across to next corner**, sc in next sc, rep from * around, ending last rep at **, join in beg sc. Fasten off. *(4 lg shells, 30 sm shells, 34 sc)*

Rnd 18: Join green with sc in first ch-1 sp of any corner shell, *ch 5, 4-bptr dec, ch-5, [sc in next ch-1 sp, ch 5, 8-bptr dec, ch 5] across to next corner**, sc in next ch-1 sp, rep from * around, ending last rep at **, join in beg sc. *(4 4-bptr dec, 34 8-bptr dec, 38 sc)*

Rnd 19: Ch 1, sc in first sc, *lg shell in top of next 4-bptr dec, [sc in next sc, sm shell in top of next 8-bptr dec] across to next corner**, sc in next sc, rep from * around, ending last rep at **, join in beg sc. Fasten off. *(4 lg shells, 34 sm shells, 38 sc)*

Rnds 20–44: [Rep rnds 10–19 consecutively] 3 times, ending last rep with rnd 14. At end of last rnd, fasten off. ■

Little Bit of Lovely

SKILL LEVEL

INTERMEDIATE

FINISHED SIZES

Instructions given for ladies' small; changes for medium and large are in [ ].

MATERIALS

- Filatura Di Crosa Luxury fine (sport) weight silk yarn (1¾ oz/160 yds/ 50g per ball):
  3 balls #008 light khaki
  2 balls each #007 light peach, #006 silver gray, #038 coffee bean and #28 light pink
- Size F/5/3.75mm crochet hook or size needed to obtain gauge
- Tapestry needle

GAUGE

2 sm shells and 3 sc = 4 inches

PATTERN NOTES

See photos for Special Stitches and How-To on pages 4–12.

Color sequence is khaki, light peach, coffee bean, light pink and silver gray. Maintain this color sequence throughout, repeating color sequence as needed.

Join with slip stitch as indicated unless otherwise stated.

Chain-3 at beginning of row or round counts as first double crochet unless otherwise stated.

SPECIAL STITCHES

4-treble cluster (4-tr cl): Holding back last lp of each st on hook, 4 tr in place indicated, yo, pull through all lps on hook.

4-back post treble decrease (4-bptr dec): Holding back last lp of each st on hook, **bptr** (*see Stitch Guide*) around each of next 4 sts, yo, pull through all lps on hook (*see photo 3 on page 4*).

8-back post treble decrease (8-bptr dec): Holding back last lp of each st on hook, bptr around each of next 4 sts*, sk sc between shells and working on next shell, rep between * once, yo, pull through all lps on hook (*see photo 4 on page 5*).

Large shell (lg shell): (4 tr, {ch 1, 4 tr} twice) in place indicated.

Small shell (sm shell): (4 tr, ch 1, 4 tr) in place indicated.

INSTRUCTIONS
SHRUG
BACK

Rnd 1: Beg in center, with khaki, ch 5, sl st in first ch to form ring, ch 1, [sc in ring, ch 5, **4-tr cl** (*see Special Stitches*) in ring, ch 5] 4 times, **join** (*see Pattern Notes*) in beg sc. (*4 cls, 4 sc, 8 ch-5 sps*)

Rnd 2: Ch 1, sc in first sc, [ch 2, **lg shell** (*see Special Stitches*) in top of next 4-tr cl, ch 2, sc in next sc] 3 times, ch 2, lg shell in top of last 4-tr cl, ch 2, join in beg sc. Fasten off. Ch-2 sps are used on rnd 2 only to give added height. They will not be worked into or used on any subsequent rnds. (*4 lg shells, 4 sc, 8 ch-2 sps*)

Rnd 3: Join light peach with sc in first ch-1 sp of any lg shell, *ch 5, **4-bptr dec** (*see Special Stitches*), ch 5, sc in next ch-1 sp, ch 5, **8-bptr dec** (*see Special Stitches*), ch 5**, sc in next ch-1 sp, rep from * around, ending last rep at **, join in beg sc. (*4 4-bptr dec, 4 8-bptr dec, 8 sc*)

Rnd 4: Ch 1, sc in first sc, *lg shell in top of next 4-bptr dec (*center 4-tr group of each lg shell is corner*), sc in next sc, **sm shell** (*see Special Stitches*) in top of next 8-bptr dec, sc in next sc, rep from * 3 times, lg shell in top of next 4-bptr dec, sc in next sc, sm shell in top of next 8-bptr dec, join in beg sc. Fasten off. (*4 lg shells, 4 sm shells, 8 sc*) Center 4-tr group of each lg shell is corner.

Rnd 5: Join coffee bean with sc in first ch-1 sp of any corner shell, *ch 5, 4-bptr dec, ch 5, sc in next ch-1 sp, ch 5, 8-bptr dec, ch 5, sc in next ch-1 sp, ch 5, 8-bptr dec, ch 5**, sc in next ch-1 sp, rep from * around, ending last rep at **, join in beg sc.

Rnd 6: Ch 1, sc in first sc, *lg shell in top of next 4-bptr dec, sc in next sc, sm shell in top of next 8-bptr dec, sc in next sc, sm shell in top of next 8-bptr dec**, sc in next sc, rep from * around, ending last rep at **, join in beg sc. Fasten off. (*4 lg shells, 8 sm shells, 12 sc*)

Rnd 7: Join light pink with sc in first ch-1 sp of any corner shell, *ch 5, 4-bptr dec, ch 5, [sc in next ch-1 sp, ch 5, 8-bptr dec, ch 5] across** to next corner, sc in next ch-1 sp, rep from * around, ending last rep at **, join in beg sc. (*4 4-bptr dec, 12 8-bptr dec, 16 sc*)

Rnd 8: Ch 1, sc in first sc, *lg shell in top of next 4-bptr dec, [sc in next sc, sm shell in top of next 8-bptr dec] 3 times**, sc in next sc, rep from * around, ending last rep at **, join in beg sc. Fasten off. (*4 lg shells, 12 sm shells, 16 sc*)

Rnd 9: Join gray with sc in first ch-1 sp of any lg shell, *ch 5, 4-bptr dec, ch 5, [sc in next ch-1 sp, ch 5, 8-bptr dec, ch 5] across** to next corner, sc in next ch-1 sp, rep from * around, ending last rep at **, join in beg sc. (*4 4-bptr dec, 16 8-bptr dec, 20 sc*)

Rnd 10: Ch 1, sc in first sc, *lg shell in top of next 4-bptr dec, [sc in next sc, sm shell in top of next 8-bptr dec] across** to next 4-bptr dec, sc in next sc, rep from * around, ending last rep at **, join in beg sc. Fasten off. (*4 lg shells, 16 sm shells, 20 sc*)

Rnds 11 & 12: With khaki, rep rnds 9 and 10. (*4 lg shells, 20 sm shells and 24 sc at end of last rnd*)

MEDIUM & LARGE SIZES ONLY

Rnds [13–14, 13–14]: With light peach, rep rnds 9 and 10. (*[4 lg shells, 24 sm shells and 28 sc] at end of last rnd*)

LARGE SIZE ONLY

Rnds [15–16]: With coffee bean, rep rnds 9 and 10. (*[4 lg shells and 28 sm shells] at end of last rnd*)

ALL SIZES
LEFT SIDE SHAPING

Row 13 [15, 17]: Now working in rows, **join next color in sequence** (*see Pattern Notes*) with sc in first ch-1 sp of any lg shell, ch 5, 4-bptr dec, ch 5, [sc in next sc, ch 5, work 8-bptr dec, ch 5] 6 [7, 8] times, sc in next sc, ch 5, 4-bptr dec, tr in next ch-1 sp, leaving rem sts unworked, turn. (*6 [7, 8] 8-bptr dec, 2 [2, 2] 4-bptr dec*)

Row 14 [16, 18]: Ch 1, sc in first tr, ch 4, 4 tr in top of first 4-bptr dec, sc in next sc, [sm shell in top of next 8-bptr dec, sc in next sc] 6 [7, 8] times, 4 tr in top of last 4-bptr dec, tr in next ch-5 sp, turn. Fasten off. *(6 [7, 8] sm shells, 2 [2, 2] 4-tr groups)*

Row 15 [17, 19]: Sk first 4-tr group and next 3 sm shells, join next color in sequence with sc in ch-1 sp of next sm shell, [8-bptr dec, sc in next ch sp] 3 [4, 5] times, working last sc in ch-4 sp at beg of row 14 [16, 18]. Fasten off. *(3 [4, 5] 8-bptr dec, 4 [5, 6] sc)*

RIGHT SIDE SHAPING

Row 13 [15, 17]: Join next color in sequence with sc in first ch-1 sp of lg shell on opposite side of Back, ch 5, 4-bptr dec, ch 5, [sc in next ch-1 sp, ch 5, 8-bptr dec, ch 5] 6 [7, 8] times, sc in next ch-1 sp, ch-5, 4-bptr cl, tr in next ch-1 sp, leaving rem sts unworked, turn. *(6 [7, 8] 8-bptr dec, 2 [2, 2] 4-bptr dec)*

Row 14 [16, 18]: Rep row 14 [16, 18] of Left Side Shaping.

Row 15 [17, 19]: Join next color in sequence with sc in top of last tr, ch 5, [8-bptr dec, sc in next ch-1 sp] 3 [4, 5] times, leaving rem shells unworked, turn. *(3 [4, 5] 8-bptr dec, 4 [5, 6] sc)*

FIRST UNDERARM GUSSET SHAPING

Row 16 [18, 20]: Ch 1, sc in first sc, [sm shell in top of next 8-bptr dec, sc in next sc] twice, leaving rem sts unworked. Fasten off. Side shaping will appear uneven on Back until Front pieces are made. Matching shaping will be on Left Front.

RIGHT FRONT

Rnd 1: With light peach, ch 72 [82, 92] sc in 2nd ch from hook, [sk next 4 chs, sm shell in next ch, sk next 4 chs, sc in next ch] 7 [8, 9] times, working on opposite side of ch, sk next 4 chs, sm shell in next ch *(same ch as sm shell on opposite side of ch)*, [sk next 4 chs, sc in next ch, sk next 4 chs, sm shell in next ch] 7 [8, 9] times, sk last 4 chs, join in beg sc. Fasten off. *(14 [16, 18] sm shells)*

Row 2: Now working in rows, join khaki with sc in first sc, ch 5, 4-bptr dec, ch 5, [sc in next sc, ch 5, 8-bptr dec, ch 5] 6 [7, 8] times, sc in next sc, ch 5, 4-bptr dec, tr in next ch-1 sp, **do not turn**. Fasten off.

Row 3: Working on opposite side of rnd 1, join coffee bean with sc in same ch-1 sp as last tr worked on row 2, ch 5, 4-bptr dec, sc in next ch-1 sp, [8-bptr dec, sc in next ch-1 sp] 6 [7, 8] times, 4-bptr dec, tr in same ch sp as beg sc of row 2, turn. (6 [7, 8] 8-bptr dec, 2 [2, 2] 4-bptr dec, 8 [9, 10] sc, 1 [1, 1] tr)

Row 4: Ch 5, 4 tr in top of first 4-bptr dec, sc in next sc, [sm shell in top of next 8-bptr dec, sc in next sc] 6 [7, 8] times, 4 tr in top of last 4-bptr dec, ch 1, tr in ch-5 sp at beg of row 3, turn. Fasten off.

Row 5: Join light pink with sc in first ch-1 sp between last 2 tr worked on row 4, ch 5, 8-bptr dec, ch 5, [sc in next sc, ch 5, 8-bptr cl, ch 5] 6 [7, 8] times, sc in next sc, ch 5, work 4-bptr dec, tr in last ch-5 sp. Fasten off.

LEFT FRONT
Rnd 1: Rep rnd 1 of Right Front.

Rows 2–5: Rep rows 2–5 of Right Front. At end of row 5, **turn. Fasten off.**

2ND UNDERARM GUSSET SHAPING
Row 6: With WS of row 5 facing, sk first 3 [4, 5] sc and first 3 [4, 5] 8-bptr dec, join light pink with sc in next sc, [sm shell in top of next 8-bptr dec, sc in next sc] twice, leaving rem sts unworked. Fasten off.

Matching sts and ch sps, sew shoulder and side seams.

NECK & BODY EDGING
Rnd 1: Working around bottom, front and neck edges, join coffee bean with sc in any ch sp near 1 side or shoulder seam, ch 5, sp sts evenly with approximately ½ inch between sts, [sc in next ch sp or st, ch 5] around, ending with an even number of ch-5 sps, join in beg sc.

Rnd 2: Sl st in first ch-5 sp, **ch 3** (see Pattern Notes), 2 dc in same ch-5 sp, ch 1, (3 dc, ch 1) in each ch-5 sp around, join in 3rd ch of beg ch-3

Rnd 3: Ch 1, sc in first st, ch 3, [sc in next ch-1 sp, ch 3] around, join in beg sc.

Rnd 4: Sl st in first ch-3 sp, ch 3, 2 dc in same ch sp, ch 1, (3 dc, ch 1) in each ch-3 sp around, join 3rd ch of beg ch-3.

Rnd 5: Rep rnd 3.

Rnd 6: Ch 1, sc in first ch-3 sp, 7 dc in next ch-3 sp, [sc in next ch-3 sp, 7 dc in next ch-3 sp] around, join in beg sc. Fasten off.

ARMHOLE EDGING
Working around each armhole, work same as Neck & Body Edging. ■

Lavender Fields

FINISHED SIZE
46 inches square

MATERIALS
- Red Heart Classic medium (worsted) weight yarn (3½ oz/190yds/ 99g per skein):
  2 skeins each #596 purple, #588 amethyst, #584 lavender, #579 light lavender, #401 nickel, #412 silver, #3 off-white, #622 pale sage, #615 artichoke, #631 light sage and #633 dark sage
- Size I/9/5.5mm crochet hook or size needed to obtain gauge

GAUGE
2 sm shells and 3 sc = 5 inches; 6 rnds = 4 inches

PATTERN NOTES
See photos for Special Stitches and How-To on pages 4–12.

Afghan is worked from the center.

Join with slip stitch as indicated unless otherwise stated.

SPECIAL STITCHES
4-treble cluster (4-tr cl): Holding back last lp of each st on hook, 4 tr in place indicated, yo, pull through all lps on hook.

4-back post treble decrease (4-bptr dec): Holding back last lp of each st on hook, **bptr** (*see Stitch Guide*) around each of next 4 sts, yo, pull through all lps on hook (*see photo 3 on page 4*).

8-back post treble decrease (8-bptr dec): *Holding back last lp of each st on hook, bptr around each of next 4 sts*, sk sc between shells and working on next shell, rep between * once, yo, pull through all lps on hook (*see photo 4 on page 5*).

Large shell (lg shell): (4 tr, {ch 1, 4 tr} twice) in place indicated.

Small shell (sm shell): (4 tr, ch 1, 4 tr) in place indicated.

INSTRUCTIONS
AFGHAN
Rnd 1: With purple, ch 5, sl st in first ch to form ring, ch 1, [sc in ring, ch 5, **4-tr cl** (*see Special Stitches*) in ring, ch 5] 4 times, **join** (*see Pattern Notes*) in beg sc. (8 ch-5 sps, 4 sc, 4 cls)

Rnd 2: Ch 1, sc in first sc, ch 2, **lg shell** (*see Special Stitches*) in top of next 4-tr cl, ch 2, [sc in next sc, ch 2, lg shell in top of next 4-tr cl, ch 2] 3 times, join in beg sc. Fasten off. Ch-2 sps are used on this rnd only to add height. They will not be worked into or used on any subsequent rnds. (*8 ch-2 sps, 4 lg shells, 4 sc*)

Rnd 3: Join amethyst with sc in first ch-1 sp on any lg shell, ch 5, **4-bptr dec** (*see Special Stitches*), ch 5, sc in next ch-1 sp, ch 5, **8-bptr dec** (*see Special Stitches*), ch 5, [sc in next ch-1 sp, ch 5, 4-bptr dec, ch 5, sc in next ch-1 sp, ch 5, 8-bptr dec, ch 5] 3 times, join in beg sc. (*8 sc, 4 8-bptr dec, 4 4-bptr dec*)

Rnd 4: Ch 1, sc in first sc, [lg shell in top of the next 4-bptr dec, sc in next sc, **sm shell** (*see Special Stitches*) in top of next 8-bptr dec, sc in next sc] 3 times, lg shell in top of next 4-bptr dec, sc in next sc, sm shell in top of last 8-bptr dec, join in beg sc. Fasten off. (*4 lg shells, 4 sm shells, 8sc*)

Rnd 5: Join lavender with sc in first ch-1 sp of any lg shell, *ch 5, 4-bptr dec, ch 5, sc in next ch-1 sp, ch 5, 8-bptr dec, ch 5, sc in next ch-1 sp, ch 5, 8-bptr dec, ch 5**, sc in next ch-1 sp, rep from * around, ending last rep at **, join in beg sc. (*4 4-bptr dec, 8 8-bptr dec, 12 sc*)

Rnd 6: Ch 1, sc in first sc, *lg shell in top of next 4-bptr dec, sc in next sc, sm shell in top of next 4-bptr dec, sc in next sc, sm shell in top of next 4-bptr dec**, rep from * around, ending last rep at **, join in beg sc. Fasten off. (*4 lg shells, 8 sm shells, 12 sc*)

Rnd 7: Join light lavender with sc in first ch-1 sp of any lg shell at corner, *ch 5, 4-bptr dec, ch 5, sc in next ch-1 sp, ch 5, 8-bptr dec, ch 5, sc in next ch-1 sp, ch 5, 8-bptr dec, ch 5, sc in next ch-1 sp, ch 5, 8-bptr dec**, sc in next ch sp, rep from * around, ending last rep at **, join in beg sc. (*4 4-bptr dec, 12 8-bptr dec, 16 sc*)

Rnd 8: Ch 1, sc in first sc, *lg shell in top of next 4-bptr dec, sc in next sc, sm shell in top of next 8-bptr dec, sc in next sc, sm shell in top of next 8-bptr dec, sc in next sc, sm shell in top of next 8-bptr dec**, sc in next sc, rep from * around, ending last rep at **, join in beg sc. Fasten off. (*4 lg shells, 12 sm shells, 16 sc*)

Rnd 9: Join nickel with sc in first ch-1 sp of any lg shell, *ch 5, 4-bptr dec, ch 5, [sc in next ch-1 sp, ch 5, 8-bptr dec, ch 5] across** to next lg shell, sc in first ch-1 sp of lg shell, rep from * around, ending last rep at **, join in beg sc. (*4 4-bptr dec, 16 8-bptr dec, 20 sc*)

Rnd 10: Ch 1, sc in first sc, *lg shell in top of next 4-bptr dec, sc in next sc, [sm shell in top of next 8-bptr dec, sc in next sc] across to next 4-bptr dec, rep from * twice, lg shell in top of next 4-bptr dec, [sc in next sc, sm shell in top of next 8-bptr dec] across, join in beg sc. Fasten off. (*4 lg shells, 16 sm shells, 20 sc*)

Rnds 11 & 12: With silver, rep rnds 9 and 10. (*4 lg shells, 20 sm shells, 24 sc at end of last rnd*)

Rnds 13 & 14: With off-white, rep rnds 9 and 10. (*4 lg shells, 24 sm shells, 28 sc at end of last rnd*)

Rnds 15 & 16: With pale sage, rep rnds 9 and 10. (*4 lg shells, 28 sm shells, 32 sc at end of last rnd*)

Rnds 17 & 18: With artichoke, rep rnds 9 and 10. (*4 lg shells, 32 sm shells, 36 sc at end of last rnd*)

Rnds 19 & 20: With light sage, rep rnds 9 and 10. (*4 lg shells, 36 sm shells, 40 sc at end of last rnd*)

Rnds 21 & 22: With dark sage, rep rnds 9 and 10. (*4 lg shells, 40 sm shells, 44 sc at end of last rnd*)

Rnds 23 & 24: With purple, rep rnds 9 and 10. (*4 lg shells, 44 sm shells, 48 sc at end of last rnd*)

Rnds 25 & 26: With amethyst, rep rnds 9 and 10. (*4 lg shells, 48 sm shells, 52 sc at end of last rnd*)

Rnds 27 & 28: With lavender, rep rnds 9 and 10. (*4 lg shells, 52 sm shells, 56 sc at end of last rnd*)

Rnds 29 & 30: With light lavender, rep rnds 9 and 10. (*4 lg shells, 56 sm shells, 60 sc at end of last rnd*)

Rnds 31 & 32: With nickel, rep rnds 9 and 10. (*4 lg shells, 60 sm shells, 64 sc at end of last rnd*) ■

Evening Gossamer
Shawl & Bag

FINISHED SIZES
Shawl: 28 x 55 inches
Bag: 10 inches square, excluding strap

MATERIALS
- Universal Rozetti Spark medium (worsted) weight yarn (1¾ oz/ 175 yds/100g per ball):
  4 balls #136-07 soot
- Universal Classic Worsted Holiday medium (worsted) weight yarn (197 yds/100g per ball):
  3 balls #106 ebony shine
- Sizes F/5/3.75mm and I/9/5.5mm crochet hooks or size needed to obtain gauge
- Tapestry needle
- Sewing needle
- Black sewing thread
- 1-inch plastic rings: 21
- ½-inch plastic snaps: 2

4
MEDIUM

GAUGE
Size I hook: 2 sm shells and 3 sc = 5 inches; 6 rows = 4 inches

PATTERN NOTES
See photos for Special Stitches and How-To on pages 4–12.

Chain-4 at beginning of row or round counts as first treble crochet unless otherwise stated.

Join with slip stitch as indicated unless otherwise stated.

SPECIAL STITCHES
4-treble cluster (4-tr cl): Holding back last lp of each st on hook, 4 tr in place indicated, yo, pull through all lps on hook.

4-back post treble decrease (4-bptr dec): Holding back last lp of each st on hook, **bptr** *(see Stitch Guide)* around each of next 4 sts, yo, pull through all lps on hook *(see photo 3 on page 4)*.

8-back post treble decrease (8-bptr dec): *Holding back last lp of each st on hook, bptr around each of next 4 sts*, sk sc between shells and working on next shell, rep between * once, yo, pull through all lps on hook *(see photo 4 on page 5)*.

Large shell (lg shell): (4 tr, {ch 1, 4 tr} twice) in place indicated.

Small shell (sm shell): (4 tr, ch 1, 4 tr) in place indicated.

INSTRUCTIONS
SHAWL

Row 1: Starting at center back of neckline, with ebony shine, ch 6, **lg shell** (*see Special Stitches*) in 6th ch from hook (*first 5 chs count as first tr and ch-1*), ch 1, tr in same ch as lg shell, turn. Fasten off.

Row 2: Join silver with sc in first tr, [ch 5, **4-bptr dec** (*see Special Stitches*), ch 5, sc in next ch-1 sp] twice, ch 5, 4-bptr dec, tr in last tr, turn. (*3 4-bptr dec, 2 sc*)

Row 3: **Ch 4** (*see Pattern Notes*), **sm shell** (*see Special Stitches*) in top of next 4-bptr dec, sc in next sc, lg shell in top of next 4-bptr dec, sc in next sc, sm shell in top of next 4-bptr dec, ch 1, tr in last tr, turn. Fasten off. (*2 sm shells, 1 lg shell*)

Row 4: Join ebony shine with sc in first tr, ch 5, 4-bptr dec, ch 5, sc in next ch-1 sp, ch 5, **8-bptr dec** (*see Special Stitches*), ch 5, sc in next ch-1 sp, ch 5, 4-bptr dec (*point*), ch 5, sc in next ch-1 sp, ch 5, 8-bptr dec, ch 5, sc in next ch-1 sp, ch 5, 4-bptr dec, tr in top of ch-4, turn. (*3 4-bptr dec, 2 8-bptr dec, 5 sc, 1 tr*)

Row 5: Ch 4, sm shell in top of first 4-bptr dec, sc in next sc, sm shell in top of next 8-bptr dec, sc in next sc, lg shell in top of next 4-bptr dec, sc in next sc, sm shell in top of next 8-bptr dec, sc in next sc, sm shell in top of next 4-bptr dec, tr in last ch-5 sp, turn. Fasten off. (*4 sm shells, 1 lg shell*)

Row 6: Join silver with sc in first tr, ch 5, 4-bptr dec, ch 5, [sc in next ch-1 sp, ch 5, 8-bptr dec, ch 5] twice, sc in next ch-1 sp, ch 5, 4-bptr dec, ch 5, [sc in next ch-1 sp, ch 5, 8-bptr dec, ch 5] twice, sc in next ch-1 sp, ch 5, 4-bptr dec, tr in top of ch-4, turn.

Row 7: Ch 4, sm shell in top of first 4-bptr dec, sc in next sc, [sm shell in top of next 8-bptr dec, sc in next sc] twice, lg shell in top of next 4-bptr dec, sc in next sc, [sm shell in top of next 8-bptr dec, sc in next sc] twice, sm shell in top of next 4-bptr dec, tr in last ch-5 sp, turn. Fasten off. *(6 sm shells, 1 lg shell)*

Row 8: Join ebony shine with sc in first tr, ch 5, 4-bptr dec, ch 5, [sc in next ch-1 sp, ch 5, 8-bptr dec, ch 5] across to point, sc in next ch-1 sp, ch 5, 4-bptr dec, ch 5, [sc in next ch-1 sp, ch 5, 8-bptr dec, ch 5] across to last ch-1 sp, sc in last ch-1 sp, ch 5, work 4-bptr dec, tr in last tr, turn.

Row 9: Ch 4, sm shell in top of first 4-bptr dec, sc in next sc, [sm shell in top of next 8-bptr dec, sc in next sc] across to next 4-bptr dec, lg shell in top of 4-bptr dec, sc in next ch sp, [sm shell in top of next 8-bptr dec, sc in next sc] across to last 4-bptr dec, sm shell in top of last 4-bptr dec, tr in last tr, turn. Fasten off. *(8 sm shells, 1 lg shell)*

Rows 10–29: Alternating silver and ebony shine, [rep rows 8 and 9 alternately] 10 times. *(28 sm shells, 1 lg shell at end of last row)*

**BAG
SIDE
MAKE 2.**

Rnd 1: With ebony shine, ch 5, sl st in first ch to form ring, ch 1, [sc in ring, ch 5, **4-tr cl** *(see Special Stitches)* in ring, ch 5] 4 times, **join** *(see Pattern Notes)* in first sc. *(8 ch-5 sps, 4 sc, 4 4-tr cls)*

Rnd 2: Ch 1, sc in first sc, [ch 2, **lg shell** *(see Special Stitches)* in top of next 4-tr cl, ch 2, sc in next sc] 3 times, ch 2, lg shell in top of last 4-tr cl, ch 2, join in beg sc. Fasten off. Ch-2 is used on this rnd only for height. They are not worked into or used on any subsequent rnds. *(4 lg shells, 4 sc)*

Rnd 3: Join silver with sc in first ch-1 sp of any lg shell, *[ch 5, **4-bptr dec** *(see Special Stitches)*, ch 5, sc in next ch-1 sp, ch 5, **8-bptr dec** *(see Special Stitches)*, ch 5*, sc in next sc] 3 times, rep between * once, join in beg sc. *(8 sc, 4 8-bptr dec, 4 4-bptr dec)*

Rnd 4: Ch 1, sc in first sc, *[lg shell in top of next 4-bptr dec, sc in next sc, **sm shell** *(see Special Stitches)* in top of next 8-bptr dec*, sc in next sc] 3 times, rep between * once, join in beg sc. Fasten off. *(4 lg shells, 4 sm shells)*

Rnd 5: Join ebony shine with sc in first ch-1 sp of any lg shell, *[ch 5, 4-bptr dec, ch 5, sc in next ch-1 sp, ch 5, 8-bptr dec, ch 5, sc in next ch-1 sp, ch 5, 8-bptr dec, ch 5*, sc in next ch-1 sp] 3 times, rep between * once, join in beg sc.

Rnd 6: Ch 1, sc in first sc, *[lg shell in top of next 4-bptr dec, sc in next sc, sm shell in top of next 8-bptr dec, sc in next sc, sm shell in top of next 8-bptr dec*, sc in next sc] 3 times, rep between * once, join in beg sc. Fasten off.

ASSEMBLY

Hold Bag Sides with WS tog, matching sts, working through both thicknesses, join ebony shine with sc in 3rd tr of center 4-tr group of any lg shell, sc in each st around 3 edges of Sides to same st on opposite corner, leaving last edge open for top of Bag. Fasten off.

STRAP

Row 1: With F hook and silver, join with sc in sc at center of one bottom corner on Bag, sc in each st across to center of last sm shell on Side, working into 1 plastic ring, 10 sc in ring, leaving half of ring unworked, [ch 1, 10 sc in next ring, leaving half of ring unworked] 20 times, sk top edge of Bag, working on opposite side of Bag, join with sc in corresponding st to last st before first ring on opposite side of Bag, sc in each st across to bottom, ending in corresponding st as beg st of row 1 on opposite side, turn.

Row 2: Sl st in each sc across to first ring, working on unworked side of rings and being careful not to twist Strap, 10 sc in first ring, [sc around ch-1 between rings, 10 sc in unworked side of next ring] 20 times, working in sc along side of Bag, sl st in each st across. Fasten off.

Sew snaps inside top edge ¼ inch from edge. ■

Snowflake Scarf & Hat

SKILL LEVEL

INTERMEDIATE

FINISHED SIZES

Hat: 21–22-inch circumference head
Scarf: 3 x 46 inches

MATERIALS

- Red Heart Soft Yarn medium (worsted) weight yarn (5 oz/ 256 yds/140g per skein):
  1 skein each #9820 mid blue and #9770 Rose Blush
- Size I/9/5.5mm crochet hook or size needed to obtain gauge
- Stitch marker

GAUGE

7 sc = 2 inches; 8 sc rnds = 2 inches

PATTERN NOTES

See photos for Special Stitches and How-To on pages 4–12.

Do not join or turn rounds unless otherwise stated.

Mark first stitch of each round.

Join with slip stitch as indicated unless otherwise stated.

To lengthen scarf, add extra chains to
beginning chain in multiples of 10 chains,
plus 2 at the end.

When working into beginning chain, insert hook
under top 2 loops of chain to avoid stretching
chain and leaving an unsightly hole.

SPECIAL STITCHES

4-back post treble decrease (4-bptr dec): Holding
back last lp of each st on hook, **bptr** *(see Stitch
Guide)* around each of next 4 sts, yo, pull
through all lps on hook *(see photo 3 on page 4).*

8-back post treble decrease (8-bptr dec):
*Holding back last lp of each st on hook, bptr
around each of next 4 sts*, sk sc between shells
and working on next shell, rep between * once,
yo, pull through all lps on hook *(see photo 4
on page 5).*

Small shell (sm shell): (4 tr, ch 1, 4 tr) in place
indicated.

INSTRUCTIONS
HAT
Rnd 1: With mid blue, ch 5, sl st in first ch to
form ring, ch 1, 10 sc in ring, **do not join**
(see Pattern Notes). (10 sc)

Rnd 2: 2 sc in each st around. *(20 sc)*

Rnd 3: Sc in each st around.

Rnd 4: [2 sc in next st, sc in next st]
around. *(30 sc)*

Rnd 5: Sc in each st around.

Rnd 6: [2 sc in next st, sc in each of next 2 sts]
around. *(40 sc)*

Rnd 7: Sc in each st around.

Rnd 8: [2 sc in next st, sc in each of next 3 sts]
around. *(50 sc)*

Rnd 9: Sc in each st around.

Rnd 10: [2 sc in next st, sc in next 4 sts] around. *(60 sc)*

Rnd 11: Sc in each st around.

Rnd 12: [2 sc in next st, sc in next 5 sts] around. *(70 sc)*

Rnd 13: Sc in each st around.

Rnd 14: [2 sc in next st, sc in next 6 sts] around. *(80 sc)*

Rnd 15: Sc in each st around.

Rnd 16: Sc in first st, [sk next 4 sts, **sm shell** *(see Special Stitches)* in next st, sk next 4 sts, sc in next st] 7 times, sk next 4 sts, sm shell in next st, sk last 4 sts, **join** *(see Pattern Notes)* in beg sc. Fasten off. *(8 sm shells)*

Rnd 17: Join berry with sc in ch-1 sp of first sm shell, [ch 5, **8-bptr dec** *(see Special Stitches)*, ch 5, sc in next ch-1 sp] 7 times, ch 5, 8-bptr dec, ch 5, join in beg sc.

Rnd 18: Ch 1, sc in first sc, [sm shell in top of next 8-bptr dec, sc in next sc] 7 times, sm shell in top of last 8-bptr dec, join in beg sc. Fasten off. *(8 sm shells)*

Rnd 19: With mid blue, rep rnd 17.

BRIM
Rnd 20: Ch 1, sc in first sc, [4 sc in next ch-5 sp, sc in next 8-bptr dec, 4 sc in next ch-5 sp, sc in next sc] 7 times, 4 sc in next ch-5 sp, sc in next 8-bptr dec, 4 sc in last ch-5 sp, **do not join.** *(80 sc)*

Rnds 21 & 22: Sc in each st around.

Rnd 23: [2 sc in next st, sc in each of next 7 sts] around. *(90 sc)*

Rnd 24: Sc in each st around.

Rnd 25: [2 sc in next st, sc in each of next 8 sts] around. *(100 sc)*

Rnd 26: Sc in each st around.

Rnd 27: [2 sc in next st, sc in each of next 9 sts] around. *(110 sc)*

Rnd 28: Sc in each st around.

Rnd 29: [2 sc in next st, sc in each of next 10 sts] around. *(120 sc)*

Rnd 30: Sc in each st around.

Rnd 31: [2 sc in next st, sc in each of next 11 sts] around. *(130 sc)*

Rnd 32: Sc in each st around.

Rnd 33: Sl st in each st around. Fasten off.

Roll about 1 inch of Brim up as shown in photo.

SCARF
Rnd 1: With mid blue, ch 152 or to **desired length** *(see Pattern Notes)*, sc in 2nd ch from hook, [sk next 4 chs, **sm shell** *(see Special Stitches)* in next ch, sk next 4 chs, sc in next ch] across, working on opposite side of ch, [sk next 4 chs, sm shell in next ch *(same ch as shell on opposite side)*, sc in next ch, sk next 4 chs] across, **join** *(see Pattern Notes)* in beg sc. Fasten off. *(30 sm shells)*

Rnd 2: Join berry with sc in first sc, ch 5, **4-bptr dec** *(see Special Stitches)*, ch 5, *sc in ch-1 sp of first sm shell, ch 5, [**8-bptr dec** *(see Special Stitches)*, ch 5, sc in ch-1 sp of next sm shell, ch 5] across*, 4-bptr dec, ch 5, sc in next sc, ch 5, 4-bptr dec, ch 5, rep between * once, join in beg sc. Fasten off. ∎

Bavarian **Basket**

SKILL LEVEL

INTERMEDIATE

FINISHED SIZE

5½ inches deep x 6½ inches square

MATERIALS

- Red Heart Classic medium (worsted) weight yarn (3½ oz/190 yds/ 99g per skein): MEDIUM
    - 3 oz/150 yds/85g #622 pale sage
    - 2 oz/100 yds/57g each #755 pale rose and #111 eggshell
- Sizes G/6/4mm and I/9/5.5mm crochet hooks or size needed to obtain gauge
- Stitch marker

GAUGE

Size I hook: 7 sc = 2 inches; 9 sc front lp rows = 3 inches; 2 lg shells and 3 sc = 6 inches

PATTERN NOTES

See photos for Special Stitches and How-To on pages 4–12.

Join with slip stitch as indicated unless otherwise stated.

Do not join or turn rounds unless otherwise stated.

Mark first stitch of round.

SPECIAL STITCHES

8-back post treble decrease (8-bptr dec):
Holding back last lp of each st on hook, bptr around each of next 4 sts, sk sc between shells and working on next shell, rep between * once, yo, pull through all lps on hook (*see photo 4 on page 5*).

Small shell (sm shell): (4 tr, ch 1, 4 tr) in place indicated.

(see Special Stitches) in next st, sk next 3 sts, sc in next st, sk next 4 sts, sm shell in next st, sk next 4 sts, sc in last st, *working in ends of rows down side of Base, sk first 2 rows, sm shell in next row, sk next 5 rows, sc in next row, sk next 5 rows, sm shell in next row, sk last 5 rows*, working in starting ch on opposite side of row 1, sc in first ch, sk next 4 chs, sm shell in next ch, sk next 4 chs, sc in next ch, sk next 4 chs, sm shell in next ch, sk last 4 chs, rep between * once, **join** (see Pattern Notes) in beg sc. Fasten off. (8 small shells)

Rnd 22: Join pale rose with sc in ch-1 sp of first shell, [ch 5, **8-bptr dec** (see Special Stitches), ch 5, sc in next ch-1 sp] 7 times, ch 5, 8-bptr dec, ch 5, join in beg sc.

Rnd 23: Ch 1, sc in first sc, [sm shell in top of next 8-bptr dec, sc in next sc] 7 times, sm shell in last dec, join in beg sc. Fasten off. (8 sm shells)

Rnd 24: Join eggshell with sc in ch-1 sp of first shell, [ch 5, 8-bptr dec, ch 5, sc in next ch-1 sp] 7 times, ch 5, 8-bptr dec, ch 5, join in beg sc.

Rnd 25: Ch 1, sc in first sc, [sm shell in top of next 8-bptr dec, sc in next sc] 7 times, sm shell in last dec, join in beg sc. Fasten off. (8 sm shells)

Rnd 26: Join pale sage with sc in ch-1 sp of first shell, [ch 4, 8-bptr dec, ch 4, sc in ch-1 sp of next sm shell] 7 times, ch 4, 8-bptr dec, ch 4, join in beg sc.

Rnd 27: With size G hook, ch 1, sc in each st and in each ch around, **do not join** (see Pattern Notes). (80 sc)

Rnd 28: Sl st in each st around. Fasten off. ■

INSTRUCTIONS
BASKET
BASE
Row 1: With size I hook and pale sage, ch 21, sc in 2nd ch from hook, sc in each ch across, turn. (20 sc)

Rows 2–20: Working in **front lps** (see Stitch Guide), ch 1, sc in each st across to last st, sc in both lps of last st, turn.

SIDES
Rnd 21: Now working in rnds around outer edge of Base, ch 1, sc in first st, sk next 4 sts, **sm shell**

The Gilded
Edge

SKILL LEVEL

INTERMEDIATE

FINISHED SIZE
14 x 54 inches

MATERIALS
- NaturallyCaron.com Country medium (worsted) weight yarn (3 oz/ 185 yds/85g per ball):
  2 balls each #0019 vicuna, #0018 spice house and #0011 gilded age
- Size H/8/5 crochet hook or size needed to obtain gauge
- Stitch marker

GAUGE
2 sm shells and 3 sc = 5 inches; 6 rnds = 4 inches

PATTERN NOTES
See photos for Special Stitches and How-To on pages 4–12.

Join with slip stitch as indicated unless otherwise stated.

SPECIAL STITCHES
4-back post treble decrease (4-bptr dec): Holding back last lp of each st on hook, **bptr** *(see Stitch Guide)* around each of next 4 sts, yo, pull through all lps on hook *(see photo 3 on page 4).*

8-back post treble decrease (8-bptr dec): Holding back last lp of each st on hook, bptr around each of next 4 sts*, sk sc between shells and working on next shell, rep between * once, yo, pull through all lps on hook *(see photo 4 on page 5).*

Large shell (lg shell): (4 tr, {ch 1, 4 tr} twice) in place indicated.

Small shell (sm shell): (4 tr, ch 1, 4 tr) in place indicated.

INSTRUCTIONS
TABLE RUNNER

Rnd 1: With vicuna, ch 172, sc in 2nd ch from hook, [sk next 4 chs, **sm shell** (*see Special Stitches*) in next ch, sk next 4 chs, sc in next ch] 17 times, working on opposite side of ch, sk next 4 chs, sm shell in next ch (*same ch as shell on opposite side of ch*), [sk next 4 chs, sm shell in next ch] 16 times, sk last 4 chs, **join** (*see Pattern Notes*) in beg sc. Fasten off. (*34 sm shells*)

Rnd 2: Join spice house with sc in first sc, ch 5, **4-bptr dec** (*see Special Stitches*), ch 5, sc in next ch-1 sp, [ch 5, **8-bptr dec** (*see Special Stitches*), ch 5, sc in next ch-1 sp] 16 times, ch 5, 4-bptr dec, ch 5, sc in next ch-1 sp, ch 5, 4-bptr dec, ch 5, sc in next ch-1 sp, [ch 5, 8-bptr dec, ch 5, sc in next ch-1 sp, ch 5] 16 times, 4-bptr dec, ch 5, join in beg sc, **turn.**

Rnd 3: Ch 1, sc in first sc, **lg shell** (*see Special Stitches*) in top of next 4-bptr dec (*corner*), mark 2nd ch-1 sp of lg shell just made, sc in next sc, [sm shell in top of next 8-bptr dec, sc in next sc] 16 times, [lg shell in top of next 4-bptr dec, sc in next sc] twice, [sm shell in top of next 8-bptr dec, sc in next sc] 16 times, lg shell in top of last 4-bptr dec, join in beg sc, **turn.** Fasten off. (*4 lg shells, 32 sm shells*)

Rnd 4: Join gilded age with sc in marked ch sp, *ch 5, 4-bptr dec, ch 5, sc in next ch-1 sp, ch 5, 8-bptr dec, ch 5, sc in next ch-1 sp, ch 5, 4-bptr dec, ch 5, [sc in next ch-1 sp, ch 5, 8-bptr dec, ch 5] 17 times*, sc in next ch sp, rep between * once, join in beg sc, **turn.**

Rnd 5: Ch 1, sc in first sc, *[sm shell in top of next 8-bptr dec, sc in next sc] across to next 4-bptr dec, lg shell in top of next 4-bptr dec, sc in next sc, sm shell in top of next 8-bptr dec, sc in next sc, lg shell in top of next 4-bptr dec*, sc in next sc, rep between * once, mark 2nd ch-1 sp of last lg shell worked, join in beg sc, **turn.** Fasten off. (*4 lg shells, 36 sm shells*)

Rnd 6: Join vicuna with sc in marked ch sp, ch 5, *4-bptr dec, ch 5, sc in next ch-1 sp, [ch 5, 8-bptr dec, ch 5, sc in next ch-1 sp] twice, ch 5, 4-bptr dec, ch 5, [sc in next ch-1 sp, ch 5, 8-bptr dec, ch 5] across to next lg shell*, sc in next ch-1 sp, ch 5, rep between * once, join in beg sc, **turn.**

Rnd 7: Ch 1, sc in first sc, *[sm shell in top of next 8-bptr dec, sc in next sc] across to next 4-bptr dec, lg shell in top of next 4-bptr dec, sc in next sc, [sm shell in top of next 8-bptr dec, sc in next sc] twice, lg shell in top of next 4-bptr dec*, sc in next sc, rep between * once, mark 2nd ch-1 sp of last lg shell worked, join in beg sc, **turn.** Fasten off. (*4 lg shells, 40 sm shells*)

Rnd 8: Join rust with sc in marked ch sp, *ch 5, 4-bptr dec, ch 5, [sc in next ch-1 sp, ch 5, 8-bptr dec, ch 5] across to next lg shell**, sc in next ch-1 sp, ch 5, rep from * around, ending last rep at **, join in beg sc, **turn.**

Rnd 9: Ch 1, sc in first sc, *[sm shell in top of next 8-bptr dec, sc in next sc] across to next 4-bptr dec, lg shell in next top of next 4-brtr dec, sc in next sc, [sm shell in top of next 8-bptr dec, sc in next sc] across to next 4-bptr dec, lg shell in top of next 4-bptr dec*, sc in next sc, rep between * once, mark 2nd ch-1 sp of last lg shell worked, join in beg sc, **turn.** Fasten off. (*4 lg shells, 44 sm shells*)

Rnds 10 & 11: With gilded age, rep rnds 8 and 9. (*4 lg shells and 48 sm shells at end of last rnd*) ■

Notes

STITCH GUIDE

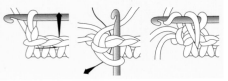

STITCH ABBREVIATIONS

beg	begin/begins/beginning
bpdc	back post double crochet
bpsc	back post single crochet
bptr	back post treble crochet
CC	contrasting color
ch(s)	chain(s)
ch-	refers to chain or space previously made (i.e., ch-1 space)
ch sp(s)	chain space(s)
cl(s)	cluster(s)
cm	centimeter(s)
dc	double crochet (singular/plural)
dc dec	double crochet 2 or more stitches together, as indicated
dec	decrease/decreases/decreasing
dtr	double treble crochet
ext	extended
fpdc	front post double crochet
fpsc	front post single crochet
fptr	front post treble crochet
g	gram(s)
hdc	half double crochet
hdc dec	half double crochet 2 or more stitches together, as indicated
inc	increase/increases/increasing
lp(s)	loop(s)
MC	main color
mm	millimeter(s)
oz	ounce(s)
pc	popcorn(s)
rem	remain/remains/remaining
rep(s)	repeat(s)
rnd(s)	round(s)
RS	right side
sc	single crochet (singular/plural)
sc dec	single crochet 2 or more stitches together, as indicated
sk	skip/skipped/skipping
sl st(s)	slip stitch(es)
sp(s)	space(s)/spaced
st(s)	stitch(es)
tog	together
tr	treble crochet
trtr	triple treble
WS	wrong side
yd(s)	yard(s)
yo	yarn over

YARN CONVERSION

OUNCES TO GRAMS		GRAMS TO OUNCES	
1	28.4	25	7/8
2	56.7	40	1 2/3
3	85.0	50	1 3/4
4	113.4	100	3 1/2

UNITED STATES		UNITED KINGDOM
sl st (slip stitch)	=	sc (single crochet)
sc (single crochet)	=	dc (double crochet)
hdc (half double crochet)	=	htr (half treble crochet)
dc (double crochet)	=	tr (treble crochet)
tr (treble crochet)	=	dtr (double treble crochet)
dtr (double treble crochet)	=	ttr (triple treble crochet)
skip	=	miss

Reverse single crochet (reverse sc): Ch 1, sk first st, working from left to right, insert hook in next st from front to back, draw up lp on hook, yo, and draw through both lps on hook.

Chain (ch): Yo, pull through lp on hook.

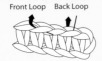

Single crochet (sc): Insert hook in st, yo, pull through st, yo, pull through both lps on hook.

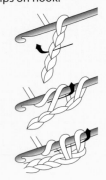

Double crochet (dc): Yo, insert hook in st, yo, pull through st, [yo, pull through 2 lps] twice.

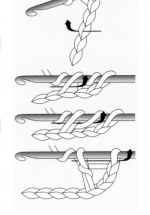

Front loop (front lp) Back loop (back lp):

Front Loop   Back Loop

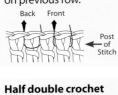

Front post stitch (fp): Back post stitch (bp): When working post st, insert hook from right to left around post of st on previous row.

Back   Front   Post of Stitch

Half double crochet (hdc): Yo, insert hook in st, yo, pull through st, yo, pull through all 3 lps on hook.

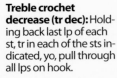

Double treble crochet (dtr): Yo 3 times, insert hook in st, yo, pull through st, [yo, pull through 2 lps] 4 times.

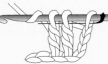

Slip stitch (sl st): Insert hook in st, pull through both lps on hook.

Chain color change (ch color change) Yo with new color, draw through last lp on hook.

Double crochet color change (dc color change) Drop first color, yo with new color, draw through last 2 lps of st.

Treble crochet (tr): Yo twice, insert hook in st, yo, pull through st, [yo, pull through 2 lps] 3 times.

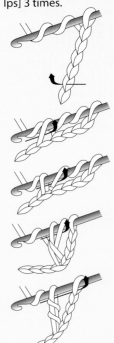

Single crochet decrease (sc dec): (Insert hook, yo, draw lp through) in each of the sts indicated, yo, draw through all lps on hook.

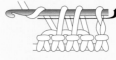

Example of 2-sc dec

Half double crochet decrease (hdc dec): (Yo, insert hook, yo, draw lp through) in each of the sts indicated, yo, draw through all lps on hook.

Example of 2-hdc dec

Double crochet decrease (dc dec): (Yo, insert hook, yo, draw lp through, yo, draw through 2 lps on hook) in each of the sts indicated, yo, draw through all lps on hook.

Example of 2-dc dec

Treble crochet decrease (tr dec): Holding back last lp of each st, tr in each of the sts indicated, yo, pull through all lps on hook.

Example of 2-tr dec

Metric
Conversion
Charts

METRIC CONVERSIONS

yards	x	.9144	=	metres (m)
yards	x	91.44	=	centimetres (cm)
inches	x	2.54	=	centimetres (cm)
inches	x	25.40	=	millimetres (mm)
inches	x	.0254	=	metres (m)

centimetres	x	.3937	=	inches
metres	x	1.0936	=	yards

INCHES INTO MILLIMETRES & CENTIMETRES (Rounded off slightly)

inches	mm	cm	inches	cm	inches	cm	inches	cm
1/8	3	0.3	5	12.5	21	53.5	38	96.5
1/4	6	0.6	5 1/2	14	22	56	39	99
3/8	10	1	6	15	23	58.5	40	101.5
1/2	13	1.3	7	18	24	61	41	104
5/8	15	1.5	8	20.5	25	63.5	42	106.5
3/4	20	2	9	23	26	66	43	109
7/8	22	2.2	10	25.5	27	68.5	44	112
1	25	2.5	11	28	28	71	45	114.5
1 1/4	32	3.2	12	30.5	29	73.5	46	117
1 1/2	38	3.8	13	33	30	76	47	119.5
1 3/4	45	4.5	14	35.5	31	79	48	122
2	50	5	15	38	32	81.5	49	124.5
2 1/2	65	6.5	16	40.5	33	84	50	127
3	75	7.5	17	43	34	86.5		
3 1/2	90	9	18	46	35	89		
4	100	10	19	48.5	36	91.5		
4 1/2	115	11.5	20	51	37	94		

KNITTING NEEDLES CONVERSION CHART

Canada/U.S.	0	1	2	3	4	5	6	7	8	9	10	10½	11	13	15
Metric (mm)	2	2¼	2¾	3¼	3½	3¾	4	4½	5	5½	6	6½	8	9	10

CROCHET HOOKS CONVERSION CHART

Canada/U.S.	1/B	2/C	3/D	4/E	5/F	6/G	8/H	9/I	10/J	10½/K	N
Metric (mm)	2.25	2.75	3.25	3.5	3.75	4.25	5	5.5	6	6.5	9.0

Annie's® *Learn to do Bavarian Crochet* is published by Annie's, 306 East Parr Road, Berne, IN 46711. Printed in USA. Copyright © 2010, 2014 Annie's.
All rights reserved. This publication may not be reproduced in part or in whole without written permission from the publisher.

RETAIL STORES: If you would like to carry this pattern book or any other Annie's publications, visit AnniesWSL.com.

Every effort has been made to ensure that the instructions in this pattern book are complete and accurate. We cannot, however, take responsibility for human error, typographical mistakes or variations in individual work. Please visit AnniesCustomerCare.com to check for pattern updates.

ISBN: 978-1-59635-316-9
14 15 16 17 18 19 20 21